Criminal Minds in Real Time

Criminal Minds in Real Time

MARK O'CONNELL

TATE PUBLISHING
AND ENTERPRISES, LLC

Criminal Minds in Real Time
Copyright © 2016 by Mark O'Connell. All rights reserved.

No part of this publication may be reproduced, stored in a retrieval system or transmitted in any way by any means, electronic, mechanical, photocopy, recording or otherwise without the prior permission of the author except as provided by USA copyright law.

This book is designed to provide accurate and authoritative information with regard to the subject matter covered. This information is given with the understanding that neither the author nor Tate Publishing, LLC is engaged in rendering legal, professional advice. Since the details of your situation are fact dependent, you should additionally seek the services of a competent professional.

The opinions expressed by the author are not necessarily those of Tate Publishing, LLC.

Published by Tate Publishing & Enterprises, LLC
127 E. Trade Center Terrace | Mustang, Oklahoma 73064 USA
1.888.361.9473 | www.tatepublishing.com

Tate Publishing is committed to excellence in the publishing industry. The company reflects the philosophy established by the founders, based on Psalm 68:11,
"The Lord gave the word and great was the company of those who published it."

Book design copyright © 2016 by Tate Publishing, LLC. All rights reserved.
Cover design by Albert Ceasar Compay
Interior design by Mary Jean Archival

Published in the United States of America

ISBN: 978-1-68319-290-9
1. Psychology / Social Psychology
2. Biography & Autobiography / Criminals & Outlaws
16.04.19

For my Lord and Savior, Jesus Christ,
who carried the cross for me.

Acknowledgments

I have to begin with thanking Pamela Jarrett of Creative Consulting Inc. for bringing to me God's message, which led me to writing this book. (She delivered the message in Atlanta, Georgia.) Thanks, Pamela, and God bless you.

I'm thankful for my three children—Jordan, Ethan, and Rebekah.

I'm grateful for my wife, Diana—who believes in me and as the commonwealth's attorney for Orange County since January of 2004, has shared the same world with me for so many years. (She continues to serve in this capacity to this day.)

Outside the office staff and of special recognition is Honorable Daniel R. Bouton, the judge I served predominantly and a rare individual who routinely combines brilliance with class. His words of affirmation have inspired me through the years, and his opinion of our office inspired the title of one of the chapters in this book.

My career as a probation officer was spent exclusively as a member of the District 26 Office of Probation and Parole—which originated in Madison, Virginia, then relocated to Culpeper in 1993, where it remains today.

Tragedy struck on November 24, 2008, when fire completely destroyed the office and its entire contents. Though we all suspected arson, no true leads were ever unearthed, so investigators ruled the fire an accident. Amid the trauma of losing all, we regrouped and bounced back.

From the time I began until the time I left, the people there represented more than an office—they were a family. Many, like me, have since retired or moved on to other positions.

Contents

Introduction 11
1 An Unplanned Beginning 15
2 Engaging the Criminal Mind 21
3 Behind the Mask 31
4 Common Threads 39
5 Pivotal Moments 47
6 A Lifetime of Criminal Behavior 53
7 The Problem with Family 65
8 A Victim's Plight 79
9 The Uncrowned Jewel 93
10 The Old Gives Way to the New 107

Introduction

In August of 2011, Ms. Pamela Jarrett told me in so many words that the Lord had instructed her to tell me that I needed to write a book. Ms. Jarrett and I met through the eHarmony online dating site. We talked by telephone frequently and eventually met in person. We chose Atlanta, Georgia, as our meeting place. Soon after we met, she said, "Mark, God told me to tell you that He wants you to write a book." Because I knew she too is a person of faith, I believed she was truly bringing God's message to me. The premise upon which this book was written is this: a thin line exists between criminal behavior (what I dealt with in my professional life) and the disciplined life (the life I chose to live a long time ago). Though she insisted that the book be written then, something deep down told me to wait. I still had four years before I was eligible to retire, and I knew I had much more to learn. I retired on May 1, 2015, and the project began in earnest.

Instead of the original premise, mentioned earlier, I decided to write the stories of many of our offenders with the hope that the reader will understand that sometimes only a thin line separates those who obey the law and those who do not. Oftentimes, that line is broken. As the clichéd-but-true expression goes, "There but for the grace of God go I."

A percentage of the criminal population spends most of their lives in the criminal justice system. Have you ever wondered what went wrong in the lives of these individuals that steered them toward long-term criminal thinking and behavior? What forces were at play? Some of the answers are simple and some are not, and I certainly do not pretend to know all the answers. Much has been written on criminal thinking; and many television shows have thrived by putting these people's lives on display while psychiatrists, psychologists, counselors, therapists, and doctors have been busy for a long time to try to figure it all out.

Some offenders meet the criteria for diagnoses of personality disorders while the majority simply has enough traits to live problematic lives that threaten the fabric of orderly society and compromise and, often, threaten relationships. From a biblical perspective, there is a spiritual component in resolving virtually every problem we face.

What this book offers is a collection of true stories from the lives of those who engaged in criminal activity and their rationale, if any, for doing so. There are so many stories to tell. Of those, there are plenty of commonalities; and yet in each one, there is something unique. I was always pleasantly surprised to find that if given the opportunity, most will offer to tell their stories (and in great detail too). However, the public often asked first.

Looking back, I know that I enjoyed the career I had. I believe God put me in that position for a few reasons. I fervently hope I made a difference. That can be a difficult thing to determine; and yet on July 6, 2015 (two months postretirement and the time I sat down to write this book), I obtained proof that I had made a difference. On that day, Diana forwarded to me a message via e-mail from a former probationer I had worked with in the early 1990s. He started a youth mentoring program and had sought the support of the Office of the Commonwealth's Attorney in Orange County. His email included these words:

> I've really come to understand the importance and impact mentoring can have on a person's life, young and old alike. I've been fortunate to have a few, unbeknownst to those who have played that role in my life. Mark happens to be one of those few. During our meetings, he spoke passionately about his faith, and he always encouraged me. It had such an impact on me then as a young Christian. I am indeed grateful to him.

I am quite certain that my colleagues have experienced those occasions when they have received feedback from former probationers, telling them that their efforts had truly made a difference in their lives. Time truly has a way of revealing the truth about people, places, and things.

In certain parts of this book, you will read about some of my personal background and experiences. I included them only to show the commonalties I shared with the people I interviewed. I have often said that if I had been arrested, prosecuted, and convicted of everything I had done wrong in life, I would have been disqualified to work as a probation officer. Yet contend that these real-life experiences were greatly beneficial to me in connecting with others and understanding some of their struggles.

I hope you enjoy their stories.

An Unplanned Beginning

> Many are the plans in a person's heart, but
> it is the Lord's purpose that prevails.
>
> —Proverbs 19:21

I NEVER ASPIRED to become a probation officer. In fact, I didn't think about working as one until I became one. Through the years, people periodically asked me how I got settled into that profession. I always told them that I had merely stumbled upon my niche.

Attending college in 1987 (later in life than many of my peers), I did not acquire an undergraduate degree until I was nearly thirty years old. Before that, I had first worked as a laborer for three years, and then I joined the army in 1979 on a four-year enlistment during which time I worked as a legal clerk and became quite familiar with the Uniform Code of Military Justice.

When I was discharged in 1983, I soon began my formal college education. In 1985, I earned an associate's degree from the local community college and then transferred to Mary Washington College (since renamed the University of Mary Washington), where I majored in history with the plan of either attending law school or teaching history.

Less than a year after graduation, I became engaged. Then in April of 1988, I moved from Roanoke, Virginia, to Culpeper, where my fiancée had already moved to. We took up residence in a third-floor apartment. On the second floor of that building, the middle Virginia Community Diversion Incentive (CDI) Program had its office; and because of the proximity, I'd gotten into contact with the program director, Mrs. Lisa Peacock.

Our early contact centered on my assisting her with organizing boxes and moving office furniture. Soon, over the course of our conversations, she mentioned that her office had an opening for a case manager and encouraged me to apply. So I applied and was offered the job in September of 1988.

The CDI Program was very much similar to adult probation in the sense that supervision is provided to offenders, but referrals were limited to nonviolent offenders. Intensive supervision and the completion of community service hours were also emphasized.

I was soon assigned the referrals from both the Orange County General District and circuit courts. In the latter, the late Honorable Lloyd C. Sullenberger presided and demanded excellence from all court personnel. I had very little communication with him outside of court. Extending words of affirmation was not his strong suit, but I always knew when I gained his approval or disapproval.

A year and a half as a case manager for the CDI Program, I'd gained the opportunity to work for the probation office.

Following an afternoon docket of cases in the Orange County Circuit Court, I walked out in the company of the chief probation officer, Mr. Alan Rasmussen.

He turned to me and asked, "When are you going to leave CDI and work for me?"

I immediately replied, "I guess as soon as I am asked."

"I have a position opening up soon, and you should apply for it."

(A new position had been created in response to all the criminal activity involving the sale of cocaine at an area in Gordonsville known as The Wall.)

I was hired on April 1, 1990. Like my assignment with the CDI Program, I began working the Orange County Circuit Court. After my first appearance in my new position, Judge Sullenberger, following a recess, looked over at me and said in a somewhat-gruff voice, "Mr. O'Connell, I need to see you in my chambers." That command triggered the same emotion I once felt as an elementary school student when a teacher said, "Go to the principal's office."

One of the local attorneys had been sitting with me in court and was present when Judge Sullenberger summoned me. I must have had a look of fear on my face because he smiled and said to me, "I don't think this means what you think it does."

He was right.

I walked into Judge Sullenberger's chambers; and he calmly said, "Mr. O'Connell, you did an excellent job as a case manager for CDI, and I don't have any reason to think you won't do the same as a probation officer."

Oh, the power of words! And from a judge who commanded the respect of so many people and who never doled out compliments casually! The words of affirmation were so timely too; they tended to accelerate my course and put my confidence level where it needed to be. They That moment brought to mind one of my favorite verses in scripture:

> Like apples of gold in settings of silver is a ruling rightly given. (Prov. 25:11, NIV)

Words are powerful. They can build up or tear down. In subsequent chapters, the reader will see the effects of both.

Returning to my early days with the probation office, in July of 1990, one of our officers was offered a job with the federal system, which he accepted and created a vacancy in our office.

Soon that position was filled by a man who became my partner, sharing the caseload in Orange County, and who remains a friend to this day.

His name is Richard Lee, known to all of us as Rich. We worked together for ten years until he transferred to another office. Together, we were known as the Orange Crush, and we shared an office space in Madison until 1993 when our office relocated to Culpeper.

We had not worked together for very long until one day when Mr. Rasmussen (known to everyone as Alan) asked me about the whereabouts of Rich.

Just to see how he'll respond, I quoted Cain from the Bible, "'Am I my brother's keeper?'"

To my surprise, Alan answered quickly and in the affirmative, "Yes, you are."

That was one of his ways of telling us that he wanted all of us to look out for each other, and we did.

However, I quickly realized that when I quoted Cain, I was doing what a lot of people do when they are put on the spot and feel guilt. They answer a question with one of their own, attempting to redirect the point of the conversation and thereby absolving themselves of responsibility.

Sound familiar?

What many of us—probation officers, police officers, counselors, and others—contend with is trying to get the truth from those attempting to conceal it. And getting the truth is something that Alan did so well.

A part of his enduring legacy is that he taught us how to find out what is really going on in the life of someone, to be attentive, and to ask the right questions. Early on, he told me and my colleagues that there is an *art* to working as a probation and parole Officer. As you read some of the stories in the succeeding chapters, you will see why.

Engaging the Criminal Mind

> The way of the guilty is devious, but the
> conduct of the innocent is upright.
>
> —Proverbs 21:8

BY THE TIME probation officers meet with individuals who have come through the criminal justice system, those who have been charged, prosecuted, and convicted of crimes have already engaged in conversation with a number of other professionals, including, law enforcement officials who investigate crimes, interrogate suspects, and make arrests. Prior to their actual adjudications in court, defendants often meet with professionals other than their lawyers for the purpose of undergoing evaluations, the findings of which may be used by the courts.

Criminal defense and prosecution teams utilize their own experts for much-needed evaluations. Once a defendant has been convicted of a felony, or his/her case has been taken under advisement with a term of supervision and other terms of a suspended or deferred sentence, the involvement of the probation office begins. For me, that typically meant the completion of a PSI (presentence investigation) report, which set into motion my interaction with a defendant.

For each PSI, I spent at least an hour and a half with each defendant conducting in-depth interviews which covered virtually every facet of their life. Sometimes, an interview only spanned forty-five minutes to an hour while other times, on the other end of the spectrum, they lasted for three and a half hours. In the latter scenario, one interview a day was all I could mentally and even physically handle. It's from these PSI interviews that most of the content of this book is derived. These were opportunities for defendants to tell their stories and for me to write their histories in such a way that proved helpful to all court personnel.

As for the interviews themselves, what I would like to emphasize is just how critical the first few minutes—even the first few seconds—of the interview are. Many of the interviews were conducted in the jails because some defendants, based on the nature of their crimes, were held in jail without the eligibility for bail pending sentencing. Those who remained on bond after their adjudication hearing were directed to contact our office for reporting instructions; and their interviews were conducted at either our office or at the courthouses, where we had some designated office space. Regardless of the setting, the first few moments can tell us much about the tone of the interview and how it will proceed.

I remember during my youth the word *vibes* was a term in vogue. Short for vibrations, it was the term someone used when talking about the feelings they received from someone else. We get vibes from others and respond accordingly. The ability to read someone is a survival tool most develop during their formative years, and regardless of a defendant's crime for which he has been charged or his IQ score, *every individual* attempts to read or assess the person in front of him.

During the interview, it is important for the probation officer to set the tone. When we perceive that the person being interviewed is receptive, obviously the job is made easier. When the person is not, then we have to dig a little deeper and attempt to develop rapport by using the right interviewing tools.

Over the course of my career, I think I interviewed individuals who had been convicted of just about every crime imaginable. There were plenty of convictions for possession or distribution of drugs, burglaries, and other forms of larceny. There were also those violent crimes that included murder, rape, and other forms of sexual assault; and later in my career, a number of convictions for using electronic means to propose sex acts with children and any number of other obscenity/pornography cases.

No matter how heinous or despicable the crime, it is imperative to remember that the defendant is a person and that human dignity always has its place. A professional must set aside personal opinions and biases. Judge Bouton, who I mentioned in the acknowledgements section of this book, has always been an excellent example with regard to how to treat everyone with dignity and exercising diplomacy in the controlled environment of the courtroom.

Our Purpose

As for the PSI reports, the phrase "paint the picture" sums up our purpose in just a few words. As interviewers and writers of the PSIs, we are painting the picture for the judge and for both parties' legal counsel for the sentencing hearings. After the sentencing hearings, the PSI is available to institutional counselors, the parole board, and ultimately to our colleagues, who supervise offenders after their release from incarceration.

Most defendants do quite well in the interview process, and there are several likely reasons. What I think tops the list is the fact that the PSI interview before the sentencing hearing represents a last chance for defendants to persuade the court to be more lenient and considerate.

Next on the list is the fact that sometimes people just want to be heard. Often the interviewee is talking about something personal that he or she has never talked about—either because it was too painful and they have repressed the memory, or just as they are finally going to talk about something they had wanted to talk about for a long time, no one ever asked.

Of course, given the mistake of having an erroneous way of thinking while communicating with those who have engaged in criminal behavior, the interview may be yet another opportunity to attempt to manipulate and derail the truth. Still, I would not be surprised if someone had said to me, "I'm glad you asked. I thought no one ever would."

The Value of Rapport

When the probation officer meets the defendant, it is a professional meeting between two strangers. People who are involved in criminal behavior have a natural inclination to be distrustful of people who work in the criminal justice system, so why would they open up and share *personal* information to an authority figure? As might be expected, the value of establishing a good rapport cannot be overstated.

The defendant is quick to size up or read the probation officer. Am I accusatory, condescending, belittling, in a hurry, or impersonal? Or am I professional, courteous, and genuinely interested in getting the facts and presenting them from an objective and fair point of view? If the defendant concludes I fit the latter description, he or she is likely going to tell me everything I want to know. And then some. Unless…

Obstacles to Overcome

People involved in crimes often display a number of biases and negative emotions that serve as obstacles in our attempts to unveil the truth. What we often deal with are offenders who blame others for their mistakes or failures, deny their responsibility for their behavior, and claim victim status in their cases though they have victimized others. Perhaps they have even used manipulation or deceit to take advantage of others. They may be angry, resentful, bitter, depressed, and confused. Many have histories of either substance abuse or mental health issues (or both). Many come from dysfunctional households, where neglect and/or abuse were common; so needless to say, it's imperative to tread carefully in talking with them.

During the course of my career, I had three different reviewers for my reports. The first was Alan, whom I mentioned earlier in the book; the second was his successor, Burton "Burt" R. Laub; and the third and most recent was Terry "Chip" R. Sullivan.

Alan taught me how to interview and get to the truth (as it has been previously noted). Burt used to tell me that when he read my reports, he could get a feel for the person and even envision what the person looked like without knowing him/her. Chip went as far as saying this about the reports: "There's always something comical amidst the tragedy, some twist or turn that you didn't see coming, and yet you enjoy the ride all the same."

Chip kept a record of some of his favorite comments from the PSIs and presented some of those at my retirement luncheon. After reciting those (some of which are listed below), he said,

> While proofing Mark's reports over the past four years, I have read the inexplicable, things that defy logic and reason, such as a guy who called the cops to report he had been ripped off seventy-five dollars worth of marijuana. Then there is the humor and perhaps a little homespun wisdom like this passage from a PSI on an Orange County Shifflett. "When my second wife and I separated, I ran into her vehicle. She was with her boyfriend, and he was in her car. I was in my truck…It's not a good idea to bring your boyfriend to your husband's house."

In one recent case, I prepared PSIs on both husband and wife, who were codefendants in cases involving theft at a Walmart of televisions and DVDs, which they used to exchange for drugs. I first interviewed the husband, and part of his explanation for doing what they did was "We wanted to get high. I told [my wife] if I get caught, I'd go to jail for a long time. She said okay, so we decided to go."

Several years ago, I interviewed a young man who came into my office with a number of body piercings and tattoos.

There is a designated section in our report on such things. When I asked him about those, he said, "Until the second semester of my freshman year [in high school], I was the perfect redneck until I fell off a banister, was bit in the neck by [a girlfriend], and became a freak." This young man was likely more a threat to himself than to others, but it was not so with our next example.

In a case involving violation of a protective order, one such defendant did not accept the no-contact requirement. Despite the number of warnings and chances, he simply refused to obey the protective order. His actions constituted misdemeanors at first, but his persistence in contacting the victim eventually led to felonies.

Over a four-week period, he sent the victim eight hundred emails and forty-one letters. Her life became a nightmare. No court action or period of incarceration protected her from him reaching out to her. He even did so from the jail and, once detected, enlisted the services of other inmates to make contact with her. He simply could not be deterred.

In my interview with him, he attempted to control the proceedings, but we worked through it and obtained the necessary information. He was unapologetic, unwilling to accept any degree of responsibility, and uninterested in obeying the court's order. Surprisingly enough, he even owned up to what others thought of him. During our discussion, he informed me that he had been sent to a mental health institution for an evaluation.

I asked, "What did they decide about you?"

He replied, "That I'm pretty much an asshole."

That was quite a concession, but there was still no hint of repentance or shame.

Here is an example of someone who denied his criminal involvement pertaining to the manufacturing of methamphetamine, had a number of legal problems in the past for which he denied personal responsibility, tended to think he was smarter than the attorneys who were appointed to represent him (and he went through a few), but showed some insight when it came to his own limitations. He said, "I think I can change the world, but I have trouble flushing the toilet."

During the retirement luncheon (mentioned earlier), Chip declared the following as the winner for the made-up Son of Sam Award for the criminal most likely to be influenced by a dog to commit heinous crimes.

The defendant indicated to me that he "has a dog which is a mix of a chow and pit bull" and that he "asked the dog if it wanted to go raise some hell." What the defendant had in mind was kicking over some trash cans, knocking over porta-potties—little things that would not get him into trouble. "Just enough to piss people off," he said. He claimed that he was astonished when the dog seemingly assented.

Here is the next and last example until we move to the next chapter.

Personally, I have always been a sports fan. Perhaps I met my equal during an exchange when the defendant said, "I was at work. My wife was feeling suicidal. I took her to the emergency room. [Then] I popped into the waiting area to catch the football scores from the night before." Yep. True sports fans just won't be denied access to scores.

Behind the Mask

When I was a young boy, I watched a popular television show called *The Lone Ranger*, starring a masked lawman and his trusted Native American sidekick, Tonto. Working in tandem, they brought the villain to justice and then rode away, at which point, someone would ask, "Who was that masked man?"

The lawman wore an actual mask, but in the real world, some people wear masks in the figurative sense. When I worked for the CDI Program, we often had our offenders undergo psychological evaluations; and one of the primary facilitators was a man by the name of Burnette Trueworthy, who became a good friend of mine. I learned much from him.

When he discovered that I was leaving the CDI Program and taking a job as a probation officer, he presented a gift to me. It was a framed picture of several individuals hiding behind masks. He wanted the gift to be a reminder that we often work with people who hide behind their own mask, that we need to be cautious, and take closer looks. The gift was also a reminder of just how difficult it can be to rival criminal thinking. That gift, along with some other treasured personal items, was lost in the fire of 2008, but I never lost sight of its meaning.

People have written songs about this very meaning. In 1971, the Undisputed Truth had a hit song called "Smiling Faces Sometimes," originally recorded by the Temptations. One such probationer made me think of this song. In addition to preparing the PSI reports, I had a small caseload of probationers I met with each month (and more often if the circumstances warranted).

In 2007, one of my probationers, to whom I will refer as Washington, had a lengthy criminal history and some previous problems with probation. This time around, he was more cooperative in terms of reporting regularly and presenting himself in a polite and respectful manner. But eventually, he relapsed on cocaine use, and it signaled the beginning (for me, at least) of his deceptive ways.

One day, following the positive results of a drug test administered in our office, I confronted him about his use of cocaine. He answered my inquiry with questions of his own, such as, "Why would I use cocaine? I'm working and doing good" and "Why would I do that? I'm a deacon in my church." I told him, "Those are good questions, but the ones I need answered are *when* did you use it? and *how much* of it did you use?"

Because his test results were positive, he was sanctioned with weekly reporting, with which he was extremely uncooperative. He was not happy about it. One day, this seemingly calm and soft-spoken individual left a voice message on my desk phone. He said that he was running late but was trying his best to get to the office before we closed. He must have thought his call was disconnected when he uttered the words, "That son of a bitch ain't never there!"

I saved the message with the plan to play it for him during our next get-together in the presence of our deputy chief probation officer. When the day came, the three of us sat down in my office, and I played the message. The look on his face was priceless—the sort you might imagine seeing when someone has been "caught red-handed," as the expression goes.

> The heart is deceitful above all things and beyond cure. Who can understand it? (Jer. 17:9)

Much earlier in my career, in 1992, I had on my caseload a probationer (let's call him Jimmy), who proved to be the quintessential con man. His career of conning others began sometime during the 1980s. By 1992, he had already served some time in prison for fraud. He racked up a huge amount in restitution (money owed to victims of crimes) with no intention of ever paying it.

Whenever I addressed his plan of making restitution, he invariably got irritated and talked about how he and his wife were struggling to make ends meet. Once, he said, "There are times when me and my wife don't even have money to put food on the table for dinner" or something to that effect.

At the time he uttered those words, our office had employed a surveillance officer who accompanied me and others on our monthly report nights with our probationers. After Jimmy left our meeting a little uncomfortable with me for having pressed him about restitution, our surveillance officer, who was known for having a very dry sense of humor, said to me, "He doesn't look like he's been missing any meals."

From 1992 up until the last time I saw Jimmy (which was in 2009, at a regional jail where he was an inmate and trusty), there had been no letup in his criminal lifestyle. Even middle age and numerous stints in prison had not slowed him down or made him change his course. A separate book could be written to record his criminal lifestyle!

Most of the offenses for which he was convicted were for obtaining money under false pretense, felonies for issuing bad checks, forgery, and uttering. He was so prolific that we eventually dubbed him a "three filer"—meaning our office had so much paperwork on him that it required three files to contain it all. Most probationers have just one, while some are in the system long enough that they require two, but few ever get to three. Think of it as an elite group that's…not so elite.

This probationer's story reminds me some of the true life story of a man named Frank Abagnale—who, early on his life, posed as different professionals, including, a doctor, a lawyer, and a pilot. The FBI became involved; and he later went on to work for them, assisting in cases of fraud.

His life story was portrayed in the movie *Catch Me If You Can* by actor Leonardo DiCaprio. The main difference is that our probationer was not as sophisticated or as polished in his demeanor as Abagnale, but what the two shared in common was an ability to con even the intelligent. Over the years, Jimmy left a trail of victims who were never made fully or even partially whole. That, however, was never a part of his plan. That is, the victims rarely, if ever, received restitution payments from him.

Here are two examples of how a person "wears a mask" in the form of letting their spouse or significant other take the lead and speak for them.

In this first example, I will call our subject Scotty. He was on my caseload during the early 1990s, and his criminal record was extensive and primarily for fraud and larceny offenses. I recall that an assistant commonwealth's attorney simply described him as a thief.

Scotty was originally from southwest Virginia and came to my attention after he entered into a plea agreement, during which time he pleaded guilty to forgery and uttering. For reasons I do not recall, he received public assistance. Also, he had virtually no work history other than short stints at fast-food restaurants. (Given his lack of personal hygiene, that may have been a good thing for the public.)

He married a woman who was mentally retarded and from a family of rural and uneducated origin. When he came to see me for his monthly meetings, she did *all* the talking for him. When I asked him if he had been looking for work, she became irritable and very uncomfortable with the question. I later found out that the two of them had no plan for him to work because that would mean an end to public assistance.

While on probation, he committed a new felony. He was charged and later convicted of stealing an elderly woman's social security benefit check from her mailbox. Prior to the actual adjudication, he and his wife were in court before the session had begun, and she was unhappy with him. Imagine the combination of her mental retardation and hillbilly background when she uttered these words of admonishment to him: "I wish youda brushed yore teef this mornin'!" Shameless, he smiled and said nothing.

A more tragic story later developed as a result of their relationship. The couple had one child, a daughter, who was an adorable three-year-old when I first saw her. I thought,

What chance will this little girl have in life? Talk about life dealing her a poor hand.

Unfortunately, my fears were realized about a year later when she was the victim in a case of forcible sodomy and aggravated sexual battery. She is now an adult and, as one might guess, has engaged in a life of criminal activity and suffered felony convictions. To what extent the sexual abuse had an impact on her thinking and decision-making, only God can say.

Could any of us have reasonably expected anything else of her?

In this second example, I will call our subject Jay. He let his girlfriend attempt to answer most of my questions, and he became agitated when he felt me pressing him for more information. His story began during his late teen or early adult years when he became involved in construction fraud.

Reviewing his criminal history, he had taken advantage of an elderly couple by reneging on a contract, which cost them a significant amount of money. He had presented himself to them as someone they could trust. By the time I met him and interviewed him for this particular report, he had been convicted of the same type of criminal behavior and had taken advantage of another elderly couple.

When he reported to the office for our interview, he came with a lady he first identified as his wife, which was really just a term he used to address a woman with whom he was in an exclusive but non-marital relationship. She wanted to set the tone and answer questions for him. Of course, interviews don't work well this way, so I had to establish who was who and what was what. He soon became agitated and took a cheap shot at me by saying, "I don't sit behind a desk all day—like you do. I have a *real* job."

My knee-jerk reaction was to think, *And your "real job" includes taking advantage of the elderly. That's noble.* Those were the thoughts that raced across my mind, but I did not articulate those. I thought of Judge Bouton; he maintained a professional decorum no matter what the circumstance.

As our interview continued, Jay softened, became more responsive, and shook my hand as a sign of respect before leaving the office.

In the next chapter, we will examine some commonalities among several people.

Common Threads

ONE OF MY most trusted colleagues and dearest friends over the years was Officer Colleen Woodside. Beginning 2001, the two of us became our office's designated PSI writers. Our colleagues handled supervision of cases for the most part though she and I did manage a small caseload. Both of us thrived in our specialization. For me, this development in my career rejuvenated me and all but guaranteed my stay until I was eligible to retire.

One of the things I remember her saying was "They all have a story to tell." And she was right. They did and still do. She would likely agree that there are many common threads in the backgrounds of many of the defendants we interviewed. Some of those, you will come across as you read the narrative.

I mentioned Mr. Trueworthy in a previous chapter. I learned much from him—even some things about myself. He and a number of other professional counselors I spoke with through the years all agreed that about 85 percent of one's personality is formed during the first four years of their lives. If that is true—and I have not read anything to refute it—then by the time we as probation officers begin working with an offender, much of what they have done and thought has been deeply ingrained in their thinking. Little wonder one of my former colleagues remarked, "We are who we were when." And I can relate personally.

When I was about five years old, I had begun living with my maternal grandparents. I remember at some point, one of my grandmother's sisters was visiting us from North Carolina. I remember after she had been with us for a while, she and my grandmother had some discussion about when she would leave and return home. During their conversation, I interrupted with this rude statement: "I'll be glad when you do go home." Neither person appeared upset. I guess when you are five years old, you get a pass for being brutally honest.

Those rules change when we are adults—even if our thinking patterns and thoughts don't. What changes is our decision to not articulate everything we are thinking. We learn what is productive, appropriate, and beneficial and what is not.

Here is one such personal example which shows how my thinking at five was not much different than my thinking at fifty. What was different is that I decided not to say what I was thinking.

A few years ago, I heard someone say that they planned to retire soon. I remember thinking, *I'll be glad when you do retire*, but didn't dare say it. I felt like that five-year-old boy again. People in the medical and mental health fields may point to frontal lobe development in the brain and "filters" as mechanisms to help us control our reactions or what we say. Whatever the explanation, all I know is that my thought process had not changed much (if at all) in fifty years. Thankfully, how I reacted had.

Back to those common threads...One of the commonalities people share is the experience of familial dysfunction, to one degree or another. Even the most seemingly well-adjusted individuals can typically pinpoint something amiss during their childhood.

Many of the people we worked with may have had an absentee parent, an alcoholic father and/or mother, or an abusive stepparent. Some perhaps have had an extended family member, like an uncle or a cousin, who sexually abused them or maybe had been locked in a dark closet, denied food and/or appropriate human touch, or were never told that they were loved or that they had any value. Some remember the noises their mothers made when they were having sex in the next room with one of the many boyfriends who were in and out of the home. Also, far too often, people I interviewed did not know the identity of at least one of their biological parents.

Any of the above factors would have an impact on a person's self-esteem and self-confidence. Through it all, they have had to learn coping mechanisms. Were the coping mechanisms they learned healthy ones? Did they learn anything about what healthy relationships look like or what boundaries were appropriate? Most likely not.

Often, I learned during the interviews that many of the defendants who had been abused as children, particularly sexually, did not disclose this information to their parents until much later in life. Sometimes, I was the *first* person they told their story to, and I always made sure to thank them for opening up. Finally telling the story can be therapeutic, including the tears that flow from it, and I always encouraged them to seek professional counseling to continue on into the next steps.

Probably the most common thread I observed in defendants over the years was the emotion of anger. What I learned early on from counselors is that hurt often precedes anger. The hurt typically comes from an important family member, usually from the stinging blows—verbal and/or physical—from a parent.

In 2011, I interviewed a young woman who had been convicted of obtaining money under false pretense. She and her lesbian partner had devised a scheme to fraudulently produce payroll checks, and she had presented two of those checks at a local convenience store. Guarded and reserved in her demeanor, it took a while for her to feel comfortable enough to open up to me. I learned that her background was filled with abuse, including sexual abuse, by family members. This abuse significantly contributed to her decision in choosing females as partners in intimate relationships.

Beneath the physically tough exterior was someone who, like most of us, has a soft spot for something. We discovered the soft spot when she described herself as a "protector of smaller human beings who are bullied by others." Because she had spent eleven of her thirty-one years in prison, most of the time she stood up for someone occurred in a penitentiary setting and often landed her into more trouble.

Junk in the Hard Drive

How many times do any of you hear harmful words play over in your head? For example, "You will never amount to anything" or "You know nothing." Words like *bonehead* or *dummy* that play over and are what you might actually use to describe yourself because they became so ingrained into your brain that you convinced yourself that it's true.

One of my former colleagues and a long-time friend Marty Carroll and I used to talk about this very thing. I credit him with coining the phrase "junk in the hard drive." We shared much about our pasts and noted some commonalities.

My personal story includes being the recipient of some harmful words. I occasionally hear them being repeated in my brain. In a nutshell, my story, which I tell only to show that it may be similar to those told to me by the people I interviewed, is this.

My parents divorced when my sister and I were very young. Both of them remarried. Our father soon moved out of state to raise another family. My mother married a man who became our stepfather, and the two of them had two children (my half-brother and half-sister although we never thought of each other as anything but *full* brother and sister).

My stepfather was a good man and he treated us well. Unfortunately, he was an alcoholic who went on drinking binges and squandered his earnings; and it eventually forced my mother and us, children, to move out and live with her parents.

My maternal grandparents, Ezra and Mary Lee Munsey, were the only grandparents I ever knew. Without them, we may have ended up in an orphanage. I think of them as two of the most honest, hardworking, and law-abiding citizens I have ever met in my life. They were solid and dependable. They provided for us well: we never went without food, shelter, clothing, or school supplies, and we enjoyed great birthday and Christmas celebrations.

But for all their good qualities, both were unaffectionate and uncomfortable with physical touch or with showing emotion. Mr. Munsey was particularly harsh in his comments toward me and more so to my brother; his words were like daggers to the heart. My brother and I have battled for most of our lives to overcome the criticism that no doubt had a negative impact on our self-esteem and confidence.

My grandfather died in 1988, and in 2005, my grandmother followed. My biggest regret is that I did not spend more quality time with them. I came to the realization in recent years that the reason my grandfather said such harsh words to us likely stemmed from his past, which we knew little about. He may have simply repeated what he had heard as a child.

Breaking a cycle is a big part of living a quality life and preparing children to be a part of something better.

Pivotal Moments

> Start children off on the way they should go, and
> even when they are old they will not turn from it.
>
> —Proverbs 22:6

IF SO MUCH of one's personality is formed during the first few years of one's life, then how critical is it that the person be nurtured and loved and disciplined appropriately early on? I think the answer is very simple.

During my interviews with the defendants assigned to me, we always explored those early childhood years and identified who the parents and siblings were. We, probation officers, wanted to know the nature of the home environment and what the relationships were like. I often asked defendants who, if anyone, they could depend on while growing up. Most everyone can identify someone—perhaps a grandparent or another extended family member.

A few years ago, I interviewed a defendant who had been convicted of three counts of murder. During our interview, I asked him who he had been able to depend upon while growing up. He was the only person I recall who answered, "No one."

As I mentioned in a previous chapter, there can be dysfunction, to one degree or another, in every home. Why do some people end up engaging in criminal activity and others do not? Are there pivotal moments in each person's life that drive their decisions to either engage in criminal activity or to live a law-abiding life?

One of the many licensed professional counselors I spoke to told me that it can be helpful, when interviewing defendants, to ask them to identify their earliest childhood memory. He did the test with me. He asked me to talk about my earliest childhood memory. I told him, " There are so many memories to recall that I do not know which one's the earliest." He then replied, "That's okay. Think of something."

After some recollection, I proceeded to tell him all I could remember.

When I was a little boy, my mother, stepfather, my older sister, and I lived in a split-level home on Frontier Road in Roanoke. From what I have learned over the years, we did not actually live there for very long—a year and a half, more or less. Yet I have so many vivid memories of living there as though it really was not that long ago.

So to my counselor, I said this:

> I was probably four years old at the time, and I remember that I was sitting on our living room floor, playing with toys. I heard a knock on the front door. My mom went to the door, and there was a policeman. I heard him ask for my stepfather. He wanted to know of his whereabouts. I remember my mom telling him she didn't know. The policeman looked over at me, and he smiled. I remember thinking that he was a very nice person. There was certainly nothing scary about him.

My counselor laughed when I told him this. I asked him why, and he said, "And what is it you do for a living?" I said, "I'm a probation officer."

I am certain that many people would read the above story and dismiss it as insignificant to how I became who I am, and yet I wonder what might my view of law enforcement be if the policeman had scared me or acted rudely to my mother?

As I mentioned previously, our family moved in with my maternal grandparents. I was probably five years old at the time. Living with my grandparents turned out to be my saving grace. They were the people I relied on for practically everything. They had no vices; neither smoked, drank, or

Mark O'Connell

gambled. They didn't even use profanity. They were Christians and attended church every Sunday.

Both grew up in the country and worked as unskilled laborers for the most part. They had limited income, always lived within their means, and never cheated anyone out of a nickel, which leads to the next illustration of a pivotal moment which taught me a lesson for a lifetime.

There was a restaurant chain at one time called Kenney's. It was known for its hamburgers called Biff burgers. They had some sort of special sauce that gave them their unique taste. My older sister and I loved going there, and it was a special treat whenever we went.

One summer day, my grandfather took us there, and he gave me a five-dollar bill to go in to pay for the food we were about to order. (Five dollars does not purchase much today, but back then it did). I went in, ordered our food, and gave the cashier the five-dollar bill. She mistakenly treated the transaction, thinking that I had given her a ten-dollar bill. I left with food and more money than I had brought in.

Elated, I shared the "good news" with my grandfather. He immediately instructed me to take the money back inside and return it to the cashier. When I did, she was so thankful. (Cashiers have to make up any losses in their assigned registers.) The lesson was this: don't take anything that does not rightfully belong to you. I have never forgotten that lesson or the one my grandmother taught me in this next example.

Always the rock upon which all family members leaned at one time or another, my grandmother was a great homemaker and managed the family finances quite well. On one rare occasion (I was well into my adult years at the time, probably in my late 20s), she found herself in need of a few dollars of cash to pay something. She, of course, had money in the bank and told me that she would repay me. I gave her the money. It couldn't have been more than a few dollars.

A couple of days later, she tried to repay me, and I remember telling her, "You don't have to do that." She immediately replied, "A debt is a debt." She might have added that it doesn't matter how large—or in this case, how small—the debt is. It has to be repaid.

Those two lessons are at the forefront of my memory. Indeed, they were also what many of our defendants were not taught. And my grandparents were the kind of role models that many people do not have. I truly believe they made a huge difference in my life, especially in helping me develop my moral compass.

In the next chapter, you will see what happens when no such moral compass exists.

A Lifetime of Criminal Behavior

DURING MY EXIT, I was thankfully able to report that there really are those cases wherein someone made a mistake, suffered the shame of a conviction, and turned his/her life around. I remember a young lady who had no criminal record up to the age of about twenty-eight when temptation—and perhaps greed—led her to embezzle money from her employer. She was soon found out; and she went through the humiliation of the court process, during which she was convicted and placed on supervised probation.

She was obviously mortified to have gone through such an ordeal. She had never been in trouble before, and unsurprisingly she responded well to supervision. She put the conviction behind her but was not able to do so with the public shame she felt. It was so great that she vowed to never engage in such behavior and, nearly twenty years later, she has kept that promise.

Then there are those who struggle with their addiction to alcohol and other drugs that keep them in and out of the system for a while, but in time, they too move on to quieter, more peaceful lives. But near the end of my career, I couldn't help but take notice of those who had been in the system for essentially a lifetime.

In a previous chapter, I referred to my colleague and friend Marty Carroll. He remarked toward the end of his career that he was supervising the third generation of defendants. In essence: like father, like son, like grandson.

For me, counting the time I was with Community Diversion Incentive Program and with probation (twenty-seven years total), I wondered, *Why, after all this time, are some people still in the system?*

This list included a pair of brothers who had come to my attention because one of our courts had ordered PSIs on both after each had been convicted of driving after having been declared a habitual offender. The older of the two had been charged after driving a moped. His rationale for doing so was that he had been operating one for so long—without apprehension—that he thought it must have been legal. He swore that police officers had seen him ride it and had not stopped him before. In preparing his criminal history, which was *lengthy* and was dated back to the 1970s, it included a variety of offenses including three previous convictions for habitual offender. The first of those was in 1990 when I first started working as a probation officer.

The younger brother's criminal record began in the mid-1980s, and he was on my CDI caseload in 1988 for bad-check misdemeanors. After that, he incurred numerous other convictions for a variety of offenses, most notably for a sex offense which required that he maintain registration with the state police.

These two brothers, including a number of other individuals who stayed in the criminal justice system for a lifetime, are examples of people who never learn to make good decisions or those who make decisions with no real thought of the consequences. Often, their decisions are geared to satisfy an immediate need or desire, such as the person who drove as a habitual offender to the store because he wanted to get a pack of cigarettes and because his girlfriend, at the time, was too drunk to drive.

In chapter 2, I mentioned Jimmy, who spent most of his life cheating others out of money using fraudulent schemes. Crimes such as obtaining money under false pretense, bad-check felonies, forgery, and uttering are crimes of moral turpitude—which include lying, cheating, and stealing. He lied to people about his intentions, cheated them in the process, stole their money, and never had any plan of ever making it right.

Several years ago, I prepared a PSI on an individual who, when I put together his criminal history, had reached a rare pinnacle in criminal history with exactly one hundred entries on his record. His offenses were mainly what we can call nuisance offenses. They included failure to appear in court, drunk in public, failure to carry registration, fictitious plates, counterfeit inspection, failure to pay court costs/fines, trespassing, and no operator's license. These were the sorts of things that made him well-known to the local police but did not constitute serious threats to other individuals.

His behavior did sometimes rise to the level of a felony, and when it did so, he was convicted and placed on probation. Our office had him on supervision a number of times. He was one of the hardest individuals to supervise because even the simplest things in life turned out to be inexplicable endeavors and annoyances to other people.

We always knew when we saw him, he would be in some self-styled crisis, and often the "crisis" arose from his inability to get along with others or simply manage his affairs, such as taking care of his basic needs. He enjoyed an audience, which would listen at length to his problems, real or imagined. He often complained of numerous physical maladies, literally from head to toe. If given a forum, he could talk all day about all the medical issues in his life and how the system was just not addressing his needs properly or how law enforcement was picking on him. Judge Bouton put him to the test in court one day. He allowed him to enumerate all the things that were wrong, from head to toe. It became readily known to everyone listening what the defendant was trying to do: solicit sympathy from anyone who would listen. Unfortunately for him, his reputation in the community was well known, and he lacked any and all credibility.

I could provide numerous examples of probationers who blame others, particularly the probation officer, for their failures on probation. What strikes me as the most interesting facet of this denial is the way in which some people express themselves. One case that comes to mind is "Joe," who like many others spent most of his life running afoul of the law. A couple of years ago, he was back under our auspices, and Officer Woodside was assigned to write his PSI report. At that time, Joe had turned sixty-six. He is someone who had been under the supervision of our office several times in the past, and his case had been assigned to various officers at different times.

In 1994, it was *my* turn. He relapsed on cocaine and failed to report often enough that eventually I requested a Show Cause Summons for violation of probation. After he appeared in court and was found in violation of his probation, he served a portion of his sentence and was released back onto probation. When he returned to the office and saw me, he immediately said, "You're the one who violated me." Technically, he would have been correct if he had instead said, "You are the probation officer who returned my case to court because I violated a number of my probation conditions."

To his credit, he did avoid using profanity in his discourse with the probation office. However, one such individual, to whom I will refer as Donny, did not. This individual began his criminal career as a juvenile with a number of burglary and larceny convictions. In conjunction with his criminal involvement, he also developed an addiction to alcohol early on, which carried on well into his adult life.

A number of previous probation officers worked with him before I had my turn (likely in 1995, if my memory serves me well). He had been paroled with the special condition that he be released directly from prison into an inpatient treatment program located in our jurisdiction. I went there to sign him onto both parole and probation.

He presented himself well because he was sober. But staying sober was not something he did for very long. He soon gained access to alcohol and violated the program's rules, and we initiated preliminary parole violation proceedings. Ultimately, he was found in violation of his parole, served another period of time, and was once more released.

We picked up the supervision trail again a year or two later. This time, released to a home plan with his father, he hoped to do better. And he did but for only a short period of time. Ordered to refrain from the use and possession of alcohol, this was a special condition of both parole and probation with which he never complied. Once more, he failed on parole, and his case was returned to the parole board.

I recall that he was later released during the early part of 1999. This time he had no home plan, and our office had to make arrangements to assist in providing some temporary shelter. I was tasked with this assignment, and I worked hard to make it all happen. Staff members of the Department of Corrections dropped him off at our office, and we scrambled to make accommodations for him. I remember personally transporting him to several different places, including a grocery store. That night, thanks to the efforts of our office, he had a warm bed at a local motel room to sleep in.

All the effort at assisting him did not bother me. What later on bothered me was that the more I did, the more he expected and the less grateful—actually even more entitled—he seemed. In a rare instance of emotion, he saw a part of me he had never seen, and he admitted that it scared him. But it might have been a good thing, for he realized that he had pushed me to the limit.

He said, "Mark, I ain't never seen you this way. You're scaring me."

I realized how angry I could personally become when, despite our efforts, the other person feels entitled rather than grateful. He never even uttered a simple thank-you, and I think this bothered me because it was all that I asked for.

His pattern of criminal behavior, coupled with the abuse of alcohol, soon began again; and this time he was arrested for new felony charges of burglary and grand larceny, held in jail without eligibility for bail, and convicted. The court ordered a

Mark O'Connell

PSI report, and it was my job to complete it. What happened next is something I will never forget because I don't think anything else compares to it.

When I went to the jail to interview him, the staff put me in what we called the old contact room. In this room, we could see outside the door into the hallway, where an inmate would be led into the room. Waiting, I soon looked up and saw Donny being escorted to the interview room. He looked in and saw me, and though I could not hear what he was saying, I knew it was anything but pleasant. Though his facial expression was one of disgust and bitterness, I managed to stay relaxed.

The door then opened, and he immediately went into a vulgar tirade. The first words out of his mouth were "Mark O'Connell, get the f—— out of my f—— face! Motherf——, what the f—— do you want?" He reluctantly took a seat, and his hostility continued. I maintained eye contact, had a partial smile, and waited for him to finish his vulgar ranting.

After a while, he calmed down some. Unlike most interviews, this one began with an adversarial tone and hostility. Plus, the sequence from page 1 to page 10 was altered as well. Still, the interview did go forward, and he unwittingly began to provide information that was useful to completing the report. Though we began in a section which normally comes later, I was able to elicit all the information that I needed to complete the report.

When we were done, he left the interview room without the same level of animosity; but make no mistake about it, he didn't exactly extend a pleasant good-bye. Yet for me, it was mission accomplished.

A few days later, I completed the report and sent it out, as required, to all parties. At the sentencing hearing, it was clear that all parties had thoroughly read the report and that the defendant's demeanor and attitude toward me had not gone unnoticed. In fact, I recall the commonwealth's attorney telling the court, in essence, that I would have been justified in terminating the interview early on and advising the court that the defendant was uncooperative and that his version could not be obtained. Instead, I stayed the course, and he commended me for it.

The judge, who always took a number of factors into consideration when deciding sentence, included the defendant's attitude, and he sentenced him accordingly. Based on the defendant's attitude and his history of failure on supervision, the judge did not order a period of supervised probation to follow the defendant's release from incarceration.

That was the last time I saw Donny.

His behavior is a reminder that a defendant's attitude can run the gamut of possibilities. On this extreme, his attitude of hostility and resentment was rare. More often, people are generally cooperative, and finding something in common or exploring the lighter side can go a long way in setting the tone and establishing rapport.

While Donny was defiant and hostile, at least he did not refuse to enter the interview room.

But one such defendant did.

This man was convicted of a brutal murder and was sentenced without the benefit of a PSI report. At that time, we were required to submit post-sentence reports when PSI reports were not ordered. I went to the jail to see him. He had decided to appeal his conviction. A different attorney had been appointed to represent him on appeal, but he had not yet met him. So when he saw me, he asked me if I was his attorney, and I said, "No. I'm with the probation office." He merely said, "Probation office? No thanks." He immediately turned back to the guards and told them to take him back to his cell.

That was the only time I ever experienced someone refusing to be interviewed.

Sometimes simplicity speaks volumes, like in the case of an individual I interviewed a few years ago. He was truly grateful that I had been nice to him. He said, "Thanks for being nice. No one has ever been nice to me." He was likely telling the truth, which makes for a sad comment.

Many of our probationers have trouble in their personal lives, including their relationships with their significant others. For example, some of our male offenders are not willing to accept responsibility for having fathered a child. Here is an example of what it means to be a "deadbeat dad."

Criminal Minds in Real Time

"Billy" had been in trouble beginning as a juvenile. Early in his adult years, he became extremely intoxicated one night, broke into an elderly lady's home, and raped her. After serving a significant period of time in prison, he was released and soon after violated his parole. Again released, he became involved romantically with a young woman, and the relationship produced a child.

During one of our meetings, I asked him about his attitude toward paying child support. His response may be typical of the times, for he said, "Not if she don't say something."

And here is an example of how a probationer during our initial interview to go over the rules and plan later made a Herculean leap in interpretation, which was mindboggling. I will refer to him as Larry.

During our meeting, we discussed many topics, including his history of using illegal drugs. He admitted that he tried many different drugs over the years but mainly used marijuana and cocaine. He knew that some states in the union had decriminalized marijuana, and he didn't understand why Virginia still lagged in the process. I remember admitting that cocaine was by far the more dangerous of the two illegal substances (based on the number of fatalities associated with its use).

In time, Larry violated the conditions of his probation and was returned to court. During his testimony—and here's the colossal leap—he said, "My probation officer told me not to use cocaine but using marijuana was okay." Judging by the look on peoples' faces, no one bought his story.

On a more positive note, thankfully there are a number of success stories. In one such case, "Steven" was convicted of distribution of cocaine, converted to Christianity while in prison, was released onto parole and probation in 1994, successfully completed both, and has remained on good behavior (inasmuch as I can tell) ever since.

During one of our meetings in 1994, he explained how his new relationship with Christ had made him a changed man, and he hoped to establish a personal ministry. I commended him for this and told him, "I too would like to have my own ministry one day." He immediately said, "*This* is your ministry."

Sometimes, when we least expect it, we receive an important message from an unlikely source. Truly, we can learn something from *everyone* we meet.

The Problem with Family

> For the Spirit of God gave us does not make us timid,
> but gives us power, love and of self-discipline.
>
> —2 Timothy 1:7

WHETHER WE, PROBATION officers, were supervising offenders or preparing PSI reports, we often relied on collateral contacts (those who provided corroborating or confirming information) to tell us how someone was doing. Often these contacts were family members. They can tell us much and prove quite helpful. Yet they can also pose their own problems, depending upon their attitudes toward us and the justice system in general.

When I look back on my career, I can count more instances wherein a family member posed more of a threat to me than a

Mark O'Connell

probationer or defendant upon whom I was preparing a PSI report. More often than not, the animosity directed toward me occurred when I was in the probationer's home. This is a reminder of the truth to this axiom: "Never hassle a man in his own castle" (or something to that effect).

I never went to a probationer's home with the intent to hassle him or her, and I am sure my colleagues were mindful that a person's home was rarely the place for confrontation. But making home visits was part of the standards of supervision. The initial home visit was required to verify that the person lived where he or she reported he or she lived. Afterward, the frequency of home contacts was driven by the supervision plan, the standards of supervision policy, and the needs of the offender or the particular circumstances.

Of course, when you go to a person's home, you never know what might be going on or who or what awaits you. Will it be an angry family member or maybe a vicious dog around the corner? Or maybe a pack of vicious dogs intent upon making dangerous contact?

Here are a few stories that illustrate the subject matter of this chapter.

In 1993, I conducted the initial home visit on a probationer/parolee who had just been released from prison following his conviction of distribution of cocaine. "Gene" was originally from New York; and I was going to prepare the PSI for the court, which was to be used at his sentencing hearing.

During the preparation of the PSI, I found the interview with him to be difficult. He tended to minimize his past criminal behavior. I recall that when I asked him about his adult record in New York, he responded (in the accent of that area), "They just misdemeanuhs."

After he served his prison sentence, his attitude toward me had softened when I signed him onto probation and scheduled the home visit. What I didn't know was that when I visited, his father held no such view of me.

I recall when I was in their home, Gene was pleasant; and as we were talking in the kitchen area, his father came around the corner and began to glare at me. While he glared, he said nothing until he interrupted the conversation I was having with Gene. We were talking about a location of someone else's home in the county. Not knowing what road he was referring to, I remarked, "I haven't traveled down every road in the county."

That's when the father interjected, "You're damn right you haven't been down every road!" Then he continued to glare, and the tension in the room became especially heightened. To Gene's credit, he recognized this and did his part to diffuse it. His father then began to lecture me on what it was that I was expected do to for his son while he was on parole and probation. I recall that I was thankful to leave that home and that I never had to return.

In 1994, I had a female probationer on my caseload whose involvement in the sale of cocaine led to her conviction, and her use of cocaine caused problems while she was under probation. Collecting urine samples is a regular practice of probation officers. Generally, those are witnessed to ensure that the person is giving a genuine sample. For obvious reasons, female probation officers collect urine screens from female probationers, and male probation officers collect urine screens from male probationers.

I needed a sample from this particular probationer to whom I will refer as Patty. But because she reported transportation difficulties, I, along with a female officer, went to her home for that purpose.

Patty posed no problem to us; but she had three family members there at the time, including an older brother who made his contempt for us obvious. When he heard us talking about collecting a urine sample from his sister, his agitation prompted him to say, "Urine screen? Shit, I wouldn't give no urine screen to no damn probation officer! If it was me, I'd throw the urine on them. Piss on them."

Obviously this made for an uncomfortable situation; but we stayed the course, collected the sample, and told Patty that we would be back in touch.

Patty eventually was found in violation of her probation and served some time in jail. She was later released and completed probation the second time around.

Later on, the same older brother found himself on probation and had to change his attitude toward us and his mind-set on providing urine samples.

Earlier in my career, I had a probation case assigned to me on a man who had been convicted in another jurisdiction for sex offenses involving young girls. The man (let's call him John) came to our office for the initial interview with his girlfriend, who was obviously domineering and attempted to exert some influence in what I was doing. She tended to speak for John, who greatly minimized his criminal behavior.

He had entered into a plea agreement with an Alford plea (this stems from the case of *North Carolina v. Alford* and in essence means a defendant agrees to stipulate that there is enough evidence for conviction without a formal admission of guilt). John's understanding of the Alford plea led him to say to me, "Guilty but not guilty."

Near the end of our session, I scheduled a home visit and asked him if there was anything about the home I needed to know. He said, "No, all is okay." I asked him if he had any dogs and he said, "Yes, but they won't bother you."

When I showed up at his home, I did my usual canvassing of the area to look for anything potentially dangerous. I saw one dog on the front porch, and much to my relief, it did not appear to be a threat. I began to walk toward the house. Suddenly, I spotted a group of dogs, all on leashes. All were barking and intent upon getting to me.

It appeared that the dogs were there on purpose as they could only get near me but not completely reach me. I had to stay centered on the walkway to make sure none could actually get its teeth on me. John came to the door and smiled.

I asked, "Why didn't you tell me about the dogs?" He simply smiled and shrugged it off.

I went inside and met with him for just a few minutes. We scheduled our next office meeting, and I left. I was never to return to his home.

A similar incident occurred when I was visiting a probationer's home. Then I was to report back to the district of origin that we would accept his case for transfer of supervision.

He lived in a remote area of the county, and when I pulled into his "driveway," he stepped out of his home to greet me. He was friendly enough. But I couldn't help but notice—and keep my eyes on—his dog, a pit bull that he had contained in an area with a fence the tops of which were angled enough so that when the dog scaled it and attempted to get over it, the incline was just enough to prevent him from doing so. For as long as I was there, the dog tried desperately to get out. I knew that if the dog was successful, it was not going to greet me with friendly intentions. I recall having stayed close to my car, remembering that I had access to a steel cage if I needed it.

As has been seen, home visits pose the possibility of danger and uncertainty. But as the reader can easily imagine, family members can be hostile in other places.

An example that remains in the forefront of my mind is this one.

In the mid-1990s, two brothers were placed on probation after their convictions of grand larceny. They were convicted and sentenced without the benefit of a PSI, and the supervision of their cases was assigned to me. As part of supervising their cases, I had interaction with their parents. It was clear from the onset that their mother was the dominant parent and that their father often deferred to her and said very little.

During a couple of my meetings with the brothers, their mother tried to exert much influence. She did most of the talking for her sons, who were very immature and lacked any indication that they could live responsibly. The good news is that one of her sons managed to do well. He met a young lady who was a positive influence. They married and started a family, and he obtained steady employment and has lived a stable life since (as far as I know). The other son couldn't find his bearings and eventually returned to court for a probation violation wherein he was found guilty and sentenced to a period of incarceration.

His mother was present during the hearing, and when it concluded, she got up from her seat and headed for the door to leave. Before she opened it, she turned to me, looked me in the eye, and said (by the obvious movement of her lips), "You son of a bitch." Even though I knew I had done my job with integrity, those words still stung a little.

A few months later, her son was due to be released from incarceration at which time he would be placed back onto supervised probation. His case was again assigned to me, and this meant another home visit. I knew I would see his mother at their home, so I wondered what her demeanor toward me would be.

To my surprise, she acted more nicely at the home visit than at any other time I had been around her. She was cordial and courteous. That may have been the last time I saw her. I recall that at some point in time, her son was diagnosed with a mental disorder and was committed to an institution.

I remember clearly another case in which a parent (in this instance, the father) expressed his displeasure with what had happened in court and directed his dissatisfaction toward me. He was also rather controlling—to the point where he thought that our conversation would be one way, his way, and I would need his permission to speak.

I, of course, did not share the same sentiments.

Here is what happened.

In one of our circuit courts, the judge placed a young man on pre-conviction probation, which means that the person was under supervision but had an opportunity to avoid a felony conviction if he complied with the terms set forth by the court, which set review dates to determine compliance.

This probationer lived outside our catchment area, so the supervision of his case was transferred. The probation office that supervised his case provided a letter to the court to report of his adjustment to supervision.

I was asked to represent the probation office in court, so I read the letter in advance during which time, the judge decided that while the probationer had made some progress, the court was not willing to conclude the matter but, instead, to continue the case for a period of time. This was to monitor how sincere the probationer was in leading a law-abiding and productive life or, in other words, how sincere he really was to the court.

After the hearing, the probationer approached me and expressed his dissatisfaction that the case had not been concluded. I gathered that he was put out that he had to return to court another time. Before I could fully address the situation (and truly he should have been thankful that the court was still willing to give him an opportunity to avoid a felony conviction), his family walked up to us, and his father immediately began to take control of the conversation.

He began blaming me for what happened and lectured me on what he thought should have happened. As I was about to respond, he approached me, looked me in the eyes, and said emphatically, "I don't need to hear a goddamn word from you!" To which I calmly replied, "If I need to say something, I won't need your permission or anyone else's to do so." In retrospect, I should have said that I believe in treating people with respect, but I believe it is necessary to stand one's ground on principle and not let someone trample you.

This man's wife recognized what was going on, and her presence and calm demeanor eventually led to his calming down long enough to leave without further incident.

In 2001, there was a case where a defendant was convicted of a number of larceny offenses that involved high-value historic items. The court ordered a PSI, which was my job to complete.

The attorney for the defendant told me to be on guard when dealing with his client's mother because she liked to be in control and to tell people what to do. I thanked him for the heads-up. The defendant was ordered to be held in jail without eligibility for bail pending sentencing, so I knew I would conduct our interview at the jail when the time came. On this particular day, I had the opportunity to meet with his mother outside the court.

True to the attorney's description, this lady immediately began our conversation with the words "This is the way it's going to be…" I immediately interrupted, saying, "Actually, that's not the way it's going to be. Your son has now been convicted, and it's my job to prepare the report. I have a system that I use, which has worked well for me, and I intend to follow it." She immediately relented; and during the course of the investigation, I visited her home, where she was polite and told me much about her son's background.

Near the latter days of my career, I completed a PSI on a person who was convicted of arson and other felonies and whose childhood included incidents of cruelty to animals. The court eventually sentenced him to an active period of incarceration of four years. After the sentencing hearing, I witnessed his father glaring at me and talking about me to one of the sheriff's deputies, who looked over at me while they were talking.

Never one to miss an opportunity to get to the truth, I asked the father if there was something he wanted to say to me. He missed an opportunity to go outside and express himself, for I would have given him that chance. Instead, he chose to say something with some sort of innuendo that was lost on me. He said, "I'm talking about your dead circle." I had no idea what that meant, so I only said, "Is that it?" He replied, "Yes." Then I turned and left.

In addition to what happens in person, much of our contact with family members is via telephone.

It's unbelievable how many times family members have called to report that someone is using drugs or doing other things we need to know about, only to find out that some of those reports are not true and are designed to give the person calling a little leverage to put us to work in applying some heat to the person they are calling about.

I remember preparing a PSI on a lady I wall call Trudy, who along with her husband had been convicted of a number of felony larcenies. Both had an addiction to illegal drugs and supported their habit with criminal behavior.

As part of her eligibility to remain on bail pending sentencing, the court directed that our office conduct random drug testing to monitor her use of illegal drugs. We did as we were instructed, and the results were all negative.

During the process, a lady called me and told me that Trudy was using drugs. She didn't know I had been conducting drug tests, so I simply thanked her and gave no credence to her report. For whatever reason, she wanted Trudy to be in more trouble.

In contrast to the above stories, there were times when we, probation officers, appear on the scene as representatives of hope (and perhaps even relief and rescue) to parents and other family members who may be at their wits' end to figure out what to do with the son or daughter who was on probation and still out of control.

The best example of this is as follows.

In 1992, I had a probationer whose use of cocaine prompted our close intervention. He was living in his mother's home. I had met her a time or two and found her to be a lovely and soft-spoken lady who seemed like a loving mother.

His use of cocaine caused him to be out of control, likely even at home because at some point, I went there to find out what was going on. When I showed up, the first person I saw was his mother, who immediately said to me, "I sure am glad *you* are here."

That told me that her son was out of control at home and she felt powerless to do anything, but in me she saw someone who potentially had the power to rectify the situation since I as a probation officer have the power to arrest.

I could tell that what she said was indeed sincere by how she said it. Though she was the parent and her son a grown adult, kicking him out of her house may not be as simple as it sounds.

Her son went on to violate both his parole and probation, served some time in prison, was released, and soon committed new felony drug offenses that led to a longer term of incarceration. I think he ultimately served his sentences and relocated to Washington, DC.

He would have done well to have followed the advice and example of his mother, but his addiction to cocaine already had too much control over him.

A Victim's Plight

> Speak up for those who cannot speak for themselves,
> for the rights of all who are destitute. Speak up and
> judge fairly; defend the rights of the poor and needy.
>
> —Proverbs 31: 8–9

PEOPLE WHO COMMIT crimes often victimize others. In an earlier chapter, I mentioned Jimmy, who had spent most of his adult life committing crimes of fraud, depriving people of their money and other resources. In his case, he left a long trail of victims.

The closest a defendant can get to making a victim who has suffered economically whole is to reimburse him/her what he/she is owed. This is called restitution. Pressing probationers to pay restitution was something that I did over the course of most of my career.

For me, getting probationers to pay their court-ordered financial obligations represented an ongoing challenge. Many did not make it a priority or were indigent, had few (if any) assets, and did not have stable jobs. Whenever we looked at their financial situation, we tried to set up realistic payment plans. If not realistic, the plan would have set them up for failure.

While all of them had been quick to take from others, many were not quick to pay their debts. Many probation cases went back to the courts for unpaid restitution and court fines. Either the courts extended their probation periods so we could monitor their compliance, or in more recent years, the courts took them off probation and instructed that they make payments directly to the clerks' offices.

Jimmy is one of my most obvious examples, but he wasn't the only one to commit such offenses and not make efforts to pay restitution to the victims.

Fraud and larceny come in different forms, and I agree with one of our judges' assessment that embezzlement crimes are the most egregious.

I had completed a PSI report on a young lady who had been convicted of embezzlement but had very little prior record. I am sure she was confident that at sentencing, she would be given a suspended sentence and placed on probation. But the judge in this case did not see it that way.

"Embezzlement is one of the worst types of larceny because it betrays the trust that someone had in you and it wasn't a one-time thing for you," said the judge. "You did so over an extended period of time, and there has to be some punishment."

When he sentenced her to an active period of incarceration, her tears of anguish—and perhaps disbelief—came quickly.

Officer Woodside recognized that defendants who committed embezzlement had figured out (or possibly stumbled upon) the best way to take out a "loan"—embezzle the money, pay it back on a low monthly installment, and do so without interest.

I could cite numerous examples of people who had embezzled monies of several thousand dollars and, during their period of probation, balked at the idea of even paying twenty-five dollars per month in restitution. Given their slow response and limited progress, we sometimes joked that our grandchildren would end up growing up to supervise their cases since restitution would still be owed.

So what is a victim's recourse? Not much on the criminal side of things when it comes to monetary compensation. If a probationer does not pay restitution, he/she faces the likelihood of returning to court, being found in violation of his/her probation, and then serving time in jail. That's a punishment for not complying, but it does not put the victim any closer to getting their money back.

One of my former colleagues used to say that civil remedies were the best means to get settlements, but even then, if a person does not have any resources, how would restitution debt be paid off?

Notwithstanding their economic losses, we learned a great deal about what victims went through when we completed victim impact statements. In that process, we met with the victims in person and wrote their stories. I completed those in narrative fashion, which had their share of quotes from the victims, helping illustrate just to what extent the crimes had impacted their lives.

About a year before I retired, I met with a lady who was the victim of a larceny. The defendant had stolen her pocketbook, and the loss turned her world (at least for a period of time) upside down.

Ladies carry a number of important items in their pocketbooks. She had just bought makeup worth a hundred dollars, had the usual keys and cell phone in her pocketbook—which also contained her wallet with her cash, driver's license, and credit cards. The defendant took one of her credit cards and used it to purchase gasoline. He must have decided that the rest of the pocketbook's contents were not useful, for it was later found smashed to pieces in a parking lot.

When I interviewed the victim, she wasn't nearly as distraught as she was when the event first happened, but it was obvious that the defendant's actions had impacted her significantly. To her credit, she wasn't looking for retribution.

Instead, she was looking for intervention so that someone else would not be victimized in the future.

At the sentencing hearing, the defendant testified and showed little, if any, remorse for his actions or empathy for the victim. The judge was so impressed by the victim's statement that he asked the defendant if he had read it. When the defendant answered that he had not, the judge said, "You need to read it, and we'll take the time necessary right now for you to do so."

The judge paused to let counsel provide a copy of the statement to the defendant, who read it silently.

When he was done, the judge asked, "So you have now read the victim impact statement?"

The defendant replied, "Yes."

The judge then repeated, "Do you *now* see what you did to the victim?"

The defendant hesitated and uttered what sounded like a yes.

The judge, understandably empathetic with the victim, pressed the matter further, saying, "You don't see just what kind of problems you caused the victim?"

Eventually the defendant stumbled through the process, and the judge was satisfied to let him return to the counsel table. The judge sentenced him to an active period of incarceration with restitution to the victim. I retired before his release, and I hope that he will honor his obligation.

Back to the interviewing process.

A large number of defendants committed burglaries and larcenies of homes and businesses. Not only did they steal from the victims, but they also have damaged their homes and left the victims feeling that their homes were no longer the safe havens they used to think they were. We classify these offenses as property crimes. A victim's loss may be difficult to recoup. Consequently, many resign themselves to the realization that it's a loss that won't be repaid.

The category we call crimes against persons include murder, rape/other forms of sexual assault, robbery, and many others.

Of the crimes that people commit, some of the most heinous are the sex offenses. In recent years, I noticed that the number of child pornography offenses had risen and that some of the offenders had never been in trouble with the law until their viewing of child pornography led to their convictions. Some of the defendants had been fine, upstanding members of their communities and solid family men involved in their churches and volunteering their time to help others. Some had huge support in the adjudication process with many family members present to show their allegiance.

Of course, there were those sex offenders who came to court alone and with no support in the audience after their actions led to them falling out of favor with everyone who knew them. In those cases, the audience may have been limited to the victims who were curious to see what would happen and looking for some sense of finality and retribution.

Here are some examples of those who committed sex offenses and their reason (if any) for doing so.

In 1991, a defendant was convicted in one of our courts for marital sexual assault and two other felonies. He and his wife had just begun living apart; and one night he went to the marital home, where he sneaked in through a window at a time when she was taking a bath. He entered the bathroom and forced her to leave with him in his vehicle.

To do so, it was necessary to tie her up. With the help of duct tape, he was successful. They left and were gone for a period of time, during which he forced her to have sexual intercourse with him. He later brought her back to her home.

During our interview, he did not really provide any rationale for his actions. He simply was unable to see any wrongdoing.

In physical stature, he was a small man. His distinguishing feature was his eyes—they had a wild look of determination—and his expressions were very animated.

At the sentencing hearing, the defendant testified that despite his actions, he still loved his wife. The consensus among the people I talked to about this case was that this defendant's sense of love was of a scary kind.

The judge sentenced him to five years of active incarceration for three felonies for a total of fifteen years. As he was being sentenced, the defendant looked around the courtroom in utter disbelief. It was as if he was hoping to make eye contact with someone—anyone—who was as surprised as he was.

He did not serve anywhere near fifteen years. Back then, Virginia still had a parole system in place. I never supervised his case on either parole or probation, so I have no idea how well (or how poorly) he complied with the terms of either.

About two years after his sentencing hearing, my colleague and friend Rich Lee and I attended a training seminar on sex offenders. I enjoyed the training, and the facilitators did some skits for which Rich and I volunteered. One of the things I took from the training was that the best way to interview sex offenders was to be *direct* and *persistent* in getting to the truth. For me, these were skills that I developed over time.

Not long after this training, I recall going to one of our jails to interview an inmate who had been convicted of sex offenses against his young stepdaughter. He had been sentenced without the benefit of a PSI. At that time, we were required to complete post-sentence reports when PSIs had not been ordered.

I found out that basically what he had done was insert his finger into the girl's vagina. When I interviewed him, he initially denied any wrongdoing; but after pressing him, he finally said, "Okay. I did it one time." Had I interviewed him much later in my career, I likely would have discovered that he did more than that.

In a more recent case, a defendant was convicted of numerous counts of both rape and aggravated sexual battery. The victim was his stepdaughter, who reported the behavior to her mother. When the police investigated the case, the accused (later, the defendant) denied any wrongdoing until he was told that what he had done would be spread all over the media. He then told the police that if he admitted to doing something, it would get out to the news anyway. Instead, the investigation led to numerous charges to which he eventually pleaded not guilty. But later on, he was found to be the contrary, and then the court ordered a PSI.

In my interview with him, he talked incessantly but said little substantively. When he provided his version of what had happened, he immediately disparaged the victim and talked about her changes in behavior and her attitude. He talked about how angry and resentful she had acted. Interestingly, he was emphatic when he talked about the stigma of being labeled as a sex offender. He said that it was the worst thing that anyone could possibly call him.

In Virginia, many sex offenders are required to register with the state police. When I informed him that he will be required to do so in the future, he said, "That's going to kill me. It's going ruin my life. I won't be able to see my kids. Being labeled like this is just devastating." He said nothing about his concern for the victim.

Until his convictions for the crimes stated, he had no prior criminal history. None.

In 2011, I prepared a PSI on a defendant who had been convicted of forcible sodomy, sexual abuse. The victim was the defendant's twelve-year-old biological daughter. Her parents had divorced, and these offenses took place in her home when her father exercised his visitation rights.

The defendant licked her private parts in her bedroom after he had told her to remove her clothes. He also rubbed his penis in the crease between her legs but never actually had intercourse. He later instructed her to lick his penis which she did. He also licked and sucked her breast on a number of occasions. She reported that her father told her not to tell anyone or he would have to go to jail.

The victim went to the hospital three times after attempting suicide.

During my interview with the defendant, he admitted to using his tongue inappropriately, which included his committing cunnilingus and French kissing. He must have felt "safe" molesting his daughter because when we discussed his dating life, he said that he could not trust women and that he did not have the money to date them.

As for the victim, he acknowledged that what he did to her was wrong. But then he shifted some of the blame on her when he said, "She acted like she wanted it too. It wasn't like she was resisting. She said some things that made me keep going." He did admit that he enjoyed what happened between them.

I met with the victim in the presence of both her mother and her therapist, and we completed a victim impact statement. The victim reported strong feelings of anger which she directed toward her mother. Her therapist reported that the victim has trouble with night terrors and has the same dream over and over again, and it is of her father raping her, so she cannot sleep at night.

The victim also wrote two letters to her father. She wrote,

> I felt angry, hurt, used, abused, and broken when this happened to me…Because of this incident, I think my life has been shattered like as if a window has been hit by a rock…My opinion about why you did this is because you didn't have nobody else to do it with; so instead you picked me, your own daughter, to use to get what you wanted.

The defendant had no criminal record before he was convicted of these crimes. After his sentencing hearing and as he was being escorted back to the holding cell by a sheriff's deputy, he looked back at the victim and told her that he would always love her.

In this next example, the defendant was charged with rape, sexual penetration with object, abduction, aggravated sexual battery, and assault and battery. The victim was his ex-wife.

The couple had been divorced for about two years, but both people continued to reside in the marital home. The defendant had agreed to move out of the home after their divorce was final, but later on, he changed his mind. He became infatuated with a twenty-three-year-old exotic dancer, and he decided that he wanted to bring her home to live with him. He told his ex-wife that she could provide child care for the dancer's young son. She refused to allow him to bring the dancer to the home, and the defendant became very angry.

Early the next morning, he entered his ex-wife's bedroom, jumped on top of her, and tore her clothing off. He then grabbed her by the hair and pulled her outside the house. He told her, "Go get on your knees and be my bitch dog!" He then punched and kicked her in the stomach and then pulled her back inside the house.

Once back inside, he threw her onto his bed. He attempted to penetrate her vagina with his penis but was unable to achieve an erection. This further fueled his anger, and he began to jam his fingers inside her vagina. Every time she told him to stop, he punched her between her legs in the vaginal area. He also bit her on the breast and attempted to have sex with her numerous times over the course of the morning. The assault finally stopped at 6:30 a.m. He then made her get in the shower and wash while he watched. He eventually left the residence, and she called the police.

In my interview with the defendant, he talked about having taken a pill for his sinuses and the negative reaction he had to the medicine, which he said caused him to hallucinate.

"It caused me to hallucinate and go crazy that night," he said. "I think I was trying to make love to my wife. Something else was going on upstairs [mentally], and I didn't have control of it.

"My memory of what happened is like I was a whole lot drunk. I was hearing voices that told me to be with my wife.

They say I raped my wife, but I don't believe that. I think she was scared and felt something that it wasn't. Maybe when I blacked out, I was too rough to make her think that. I remember that at times it felt pleasant to be with her. I remember that she looked pretty."

He also denied remembering that he punched her. He said, "I remember my wife blamed this all on me. I may have been the aggressor, but she told me to do things with her. During the time, I blacked out. My mind was flashing on and off. I may have been too rough to her."

In the victim impact statement, the victim reported a number of physical injuries, but the tougher ones to deal with were the psychological ones. She reported that she continued to feel frightened and had nightmares. Despite the fact that the defendant had been ordered not to have contact with her, he had telephoned her and sent her letters.

In one of those letters, he asked if she would speak for him at the sentencing hearing. She declined and said, "I have no love or feelings for him. For what he did to me, they should keep him in jail and throw away the key. His family blames me that he is in jail."

She was seen by a psychiatrist who diagnosed her with post-traumatic stress disorder. She was prescribed medication and sought treatment on an outpatient basis.

When asked how she thought justice would be best served, she said, "That he never gets out of jail. If he does, he'll finish what he started. What he did has destroyed me. I want it all to be over with, but I know it never will be."

At the sentencing hearing, the defendant testified and, during the course of his testimony, said that based on how he had been treated at the jail and by law enforcement officials, he felt like he was a victim.

Ever alert to the testimony of all witnesses, the judge interrupted the defendant's testimony at that juncture and asked the defendant, "Did I just hear you say that *you* feel like you are a victim?"

"Yes," said the defendant, who convinced no one but himself.

These stories and a number of others are examples of how people who commit crimes and cause injury to others claim victim status for themselves, which is part and parcel of their distorted way of thinking.

In the next chapter, you will meet some of the people I worked with. They individually and collectively formed a team as capable as any to face the challenges that come with supervising offenders.

The Uncrowned Jewel

IN THE INTRODUCTION section of this book, I wrote about an individual who I had supervised on probation and parole during the early 1990s. He had served his time and had gone on to live a law-abiding life. Recently he began a youth mentoring program, and he sent an e-mail to the Office of the Commonwealth's Attorney in Orange County. In the e-mail, he spoke highly of me.

He is an example of people who turned their lives around and gave credit to their probation officers for having made a difference in their lives. Clearly this is positive feedback that all of my colleagues at some point in time have received.

But how in our day-to-day lives do we measure how well we are doing or to what extent we are making a difference?

That can be difficult to quantify, but I suppose we can look to our peers or coworkers because they are the people who see us daily and observe what we are doing and how we are doing it. My peers could evaluate my performance based on the quality of reports that I wrote, the rapport I had with probationers, and the manner with which I responded to them.

Likewise, I could evaluate my peers based on what I observed in the way they treated their probationers, provided supervision, wrote major violation reports (a summary of one's adjustment on probation and/or parole), and how they testified in court.

Outside the office, the people who witness the quality of our work are the judges, commonwealth attorneys, defense attorneys, members of both the sheriff's and the clerk's offices, defendants, victims, and other witnesses. It is, in my opinion, in the courtroom where the proof is in the pudding.

From the time I began to the present, the District 26 probation office has served four circuit courts which include the counties of Culpeper, Orange, Madison, and Greene. Judge Bouton presides in three of the four, including the two courts that I served over the course of my career.

He became a judge in 2000 after having served for a number of years as the commonwealth's attorney in Greene. He graduated from two very prestigious schools—prelaw at Brown University and law school at the University of Virginia.

Despite such impressive formal education, he is humble and respectful to all. He maintains a professional decorum in court and treats everyone with dignity. I have also seen him serve as the master of ceremonies at different events; and I imagine he would be an excellent diplomat, referee, and whatever else he chooses to do.

I always looked forward to those rare opportunities when I could talk to him outside of the courtroom.

On one such occasion, I ran into him in one of the clerks' offices, and during our discussion, I remember him saying these exact words: "The District 26 probation office is the uncrowned jewel of the sixteenth judicial circuit."

Based on my view of Judge Bouton, I concluded that those words were the ultimate compliment, and I shared them with my colleagues.

Let's trace a few steps in time to learn why Judge Bouton would come to this conclusion.

When I was hired in 1990, our office was small. We had a total of six officers and two secretaries. We soon added a surveillance officer to put the total at seven.

In 1993, our office relocated to Culpeper. We gradually grew to having twelve officers and three secretarial staff, which was true at the time this book was written.

Here is the key point: from about 2001 through 2011, we had little, if any, turnover. That was a ten-year period of continuity that not only we enjoyed but also the judge. And continuity is one of those intangibles that successful programs, businesses, and sports teams enjoy.

The world of probation is one run by people, and it takes *good* people to make things work. That said, let's meet some of the people who defined and continue to define what I will term the spirit of 26.

I have to begin with Alan Rasmussen, who became the chief probation officer sometime during the 1980s. He knew the job inside and out and was a master of the art. He insisted on doing quality work and representing our office well. He created a familial atmosphere, and the office felt like a safe haven. Part of his enduring legacy is that he taught us how to engage offenders and get to the truth.

In 1999, upper management wanted him to transfer to the Charlottesville office, where they felt he was most needed. He made the transfer and later retired.

His two successors at District 26 kept the familial atmosphere intact.

The first was Burton "Burt" R. Laub. Burt had joined our office in 1991 after having previously worked as a juvenile probation officer.

Burt has always been one of the most consistent people I have ever known: he always treated people fairly, and he maintained an open-door policy. He had a calm demeanor and did well in supervising difficult offenders. He had a great work ethic, and his reports were accurate and reliable.

In February of 2011, Burt retired.

Daniel "Dan" J. Karkos was promoted to chief probation officer, and Terry "Chip" R. Sullivan was promoted to deputy chief probation officer.

The spirit continued.

Dan and Chip were (and remain) a winning tandem, and people enjoy working for them.

Dan joined our office in 1995 after previously working as a juvenile probation officer in Culpeper. Before that, he did police work in New York and Texas. In 2000, he was promoted from probation officer to deputy chief probation officer. The consensus in the office was that he would be the person who would look out for all of us. Time has proven this to be true. Dan has a certain presence about him and has been a pillar of strength through difficult times. As a result, people are naturally loyal to him.

Chip joined our office about the time of 9/11.

It has been proven that he joined the team at just the right time.

Energetic, eager to please, a quick study, and sharp witted, Chip has been the go-to player on this team since he joined it.

Two major events occurred in 2008, and Chip played a critical role in our adaptation and recovery.

First, in October of that year, our department implemented a new software program known as CORIS, which is a web-based system that enables jurisdictions to manage offenders under community and institutional supervision with a centralized database.

Change—whether positive or negative—causes stress, and this was a major change that all of us across the commonwealth had to adapt to.

But what made it particularly difficult for District 26 is that one month later, fire completely destroyed our office building and all of its contents. Every file and piece of paper literally went up in smoke.

We were shell shocked from the total loss, but we weren't homeless for long. To its credit, upper management made immediate arrangements for us to move across the street into an office building that had recently become vacant. We began the move that very day. We watched from across the street the rise of residual smoke, and individually we later walked among the ruins looking for something that might have remained intact or have not gotten totally ruined.

Every file had to be recreated to the best of our ability. Officers periodically went to clerks' offices and made copies of pertinent documents to create files on their offenders.

Chip played the pivotal role in being our office's CORIS point person. He quickly adapted to it and shared his knowledge with the rest of us. When people had questions, they often turned to him.

Those were trying times: adapting to a new system in a new building while starting over after having lost everything. But we persevered and, just a little over two years later, we moved back to our original spot across the street after the department had arranged for the construction of a new office.

In December of 2010, we were in the best building District 26 had ever had. All was new, and the newness of something always has some psychological boost. And this was no exception.

We experienced a relative calm from the time we moved into our new office until about March of 2014. I pinpoint that specific time as the beginning of an unplanned exodus. When it concluded in July of 2015, six officers and one secretary—about fifty percent of our staff—had left, and all were on terms of their own choosing.

The first to depart was Officer Tammy R. Russell, who relocated and began a new career. She had joined the team in 2003 after having worked as an institutional counselor. She established a reputation for being a hardworking and thorough officer who took the time to know the people on her caseload.

She had a knack for getting to the truth when she talked to people, even the most gifted of prevaricators (a fancier term for liars). She wrote excellent reports and testified well in court, where it was obvious to everyone that she knew her cases inside and out and had gone above and beyond the required standards to help people.

There were occasions when I interviewed defendants for PSI reports, and their history included stints on probation. If Officer Russell had been their probation officer, invariably they spoke highly of her.

She was a team player and was always willing to assist. She was a big part of our office's continuity.

So was the next person who left.

Geneva "Pete" S. Tanner retired the following month. Our office's lead secretary, she retired after thirty-five years of devoted service. She had been an anchor whose work ethic and record-keeping methods were second to none. Her orderly and precise methods were her signature on the volume of files that were generated through the years. She was particularly affected when the fire of November 24, 2008, destroyed all. She stayed on for seven more years and made a huge contribution during the reconstruction era.

A couple of months later, Officer Eric J. Fling made a lateral transfer to another district office.

Eric had first joined the team in 2001 as a volunteer. He was later hired in 2002 and spent the next thirteen years as a solid team member who took on a number of additional duties and did so without murmur or complaint. Burt Laub described Eric as the kind of guy who's "not afraid to roll up his sleeves and get the job done."

He and his family suffered through the anguish that comes when a child is diagnosed with cancer. Through it all, Eric stayed the course and remained a team player. Like Officer Russell, he knew his cases well and testified in court accurately and authoritatively.

I am honored to call Eric a true friend. He is a loyal and forgiving person who is quick to come to one's aid.

In September of 2014, Senior Probation Officer and Certified Substance Abuse Counselor Martin "Marty" E. Carroll retired.

In him, we lost a valuable resource. His expertise on substance abuse and mental health were invaluable. He combined formal education with real-life experiences. His extensive working skills served our office and the people on his caseload quite well over a twenty-year period. With his retirement, we also lost an important component in the office dynamic that we had enjoyed for so long.

I learned much from him and submit that his initial interviews with his probationers had to be among the best in the commonwealth. Even the most manipulative and deceitful offenders would have to acknowledge in court that they understood the rules of probation because he had put matters in words that even they could understand.

He may have had as big an impact on the lives of those he supervised as anyone who has worked in the system, and he worked with some of our most difficult offenders—those with the dual diagnoses of substance abuse and mental health issues. His legacy continues because he is still in the business of helping others in their struggles.

He and I established a friendship early on and remain close friends to this day.

After I retired on May 1, 2015, the next person to follow suit was Officer Colleen B. Woodside. She joined District 26 in 1996 after previously working in the Warsaw office.

In 2001, she and I became our office's designated PSI writers.

The switch suited us both quite well. She was assigned the PSI reports for Culpeper and Madison, and I had Orange and Greene. This specialization that we shared contributed to the bonds that developed between us. We came to rely upon each other. Marty and I think of her as a sister.

From the time she began until her last day on the job, her pursuit of excellence was unequaled. Her reports were always thorough, detailed, accurate, and verified. She went to great lengths to produce such quality reports. Judge Bouton commended her for her reports, and she cherished his words of affirmation. And no matter the volume of reports she had to write, she never compromised quality.

I should note that using CORIS allows officers across the commonwealth access to the same information about an individual offender, including any PSI report that may have been completed. I am sure that a number of officers were thankful when they had the opportunity to use one of her reports as a template for theirs (I was one of them). If I had to do a PSI on someone and she had already done a report in the recent or even distant past, I literally thanked God and knew that my job was going to be made much easier because of it. I salute her for her commitment to excellence.

Soon after her retirement, another long-time member of District 26 retired and ended the exodus.

His name is Officer Walter "Walt" T. Wright. Like most of us, he had a number of nicknames. I preferred Wally.

Regardless of what one called him, the consensus was that he was a real gentleman and a true friend. He came from a broad background which included service in the navy, leading a church as its ordained minister, and working as an institutional counselor just prior to joining District 26 in 1999.

He supervised a large and difficult caseload. Using a sports analogy, if Babe Ruth was the "Sultan of Swat," then Wally was the "Sultan of Show Cause." This was a reference to the number of show cause letters for probation violation that he was forced to write.

He battled a myriad of health problems throughout the years, and he recently retired. He has taken up residence at a beach, where I hope he feels some well-deserved rejuvenation.

Everyone liked him—even his most difficult probationers. He established an immediate rapport with them.

I am thankful to call him a friend.

Among the old guard, there remain two people at District 26 who have both been there since 1997.

Officer Alessa "ACE" C. Edwards joined the team after previously working as a case manager for the Middle Virginia CDI Program. Within the last year, she was promoted to senior probation officer, a recognition that is well deserved.

Like Colleen, I think of Alessa as a sister and a trusted confidant. She has a solid work ethic and is dedicated. She has a lot of friends because she is a good friend, and she maintains a healthy balance of hard work and social interaction.

I enjoyed talking to her for a number of reasons, including her knack for quickly and accurately bottom lining something. I often compared the dynamic in our relationship to the one between Lucy and Charlie Brown (two major figures in the *Peanuts* cartoon series).

Lucy would hold the football in position for Charlie Brown to kick it. Just as he approached and readied his kicking leg to strike the ball, Lucy would pick it up, and Charlie Brown would fall flat to his back. While "ACE" would never literally do such a thing, the banter and ribbing we enjoyed struck me as similar to what the animated characters did.

Marion B. Dodson remains a part of the secretarial staff.

With a compassionate heart and the gift of service to others, she quickly became known as Mom. After all, what kind of family would it be without the presence of a motherly figure to take care of us?

Mom routinely cooked for us and for her church. She was also our point person whenever we had computer- or telephone-related problems. Without her, our office family would not have been complete. I owe her a lifetime debt of gratitude. She will always be a dear friend.

Outside the office, I want to recognize another recent retiree whose combined career as both a probation and senior probation officer spanned thirty-seven years. She served our immediate neighbors to the north, the District 25 probation office with its sub-office in Warrenton of Fauquier County.

Her name is Diane "DD" D. Moore.

Cut from the same cloth as the people previously mentioned, she would have fit in nicely with District 26.

In the course of writing this book, I, along with Marty and Colleen, had a chance to meet with her for lunch. We talked at length and shared our memories. When it was over, Marty and I took Colleen home, where she recommended that I include Diane in this book.

A couple of days later, I asked Colleen to put into words what she thought Diane had represented over such a long career.

Here's what she had to say:

> Like us, Diane valued direct interaction with offenders and networking with local agencies in an effort to change lives for the better. Like us, she valued quality and always helped other districts when called upon. She was a great asset to the Department of Corrections.

When Diane considered the friendship she has with us and the time during which we had served, she said, "We were part of the grassroots. We were pioneers."

And when I consider the people I have had the privilege to work with and the memories we made, including the crises through which we battled, I know the bonds we have run deep.

The Old Gives Way to the New

WHETHER SOMEONE SERVES for twenty, twenty-five, thirty-five, or nearly forty years, the reality is that everyone's time comes and goes. And while my exodus may have ended one era, a new era had already begun by the time I retired.

Here are some of the people to whom we passed on the torch:

Officer Lori A. Henderson joined District 26 during the latter part of 2011. She had previously worked as a juvenile probation officer and immediately began supervision of those with the toughest caseload: sex offenders. She wrote very thorough major violation reports. Prior to the publication of this book, I learned of her making the transfer to another district.

Mark O'Connell

Officer Erica J. "Lil' Red" Slaughter was hired next. I often thought of her as "A Meteor Shining Brightly," to borrow the words of one Civil War general to describe another. Well-liked and endearing, she became the office's CORIS point person.

Officer Ronald T. "Ron" Walters was the next hire, and I had the privilege of participating with him in a segment of mandated training. A good-natured gentleman, he is the office's gang specialist.

Officer Patricia "Trish" Robertson joined the team next after transferring from another district. Before that, she had volunteered her time at our office with the hope of one day joining it. By the time I retired, she had established a reputation as a hardworking officer and team player who often volunteered to take up additional duties.

Officer Barbara A. Amos joined the staff just a few months prior to my retirement. I understand she had a supervisory background. I believe I would have enjoyed working with her had I stayed.

Officer Stephen A. Smith was hired next. He impressed me from the beginning because his level of wisdom exceeded his young age. I would describe him as another meteor shining brightly.

Officer Stephanie Boteler was hired as my replacement. I had about five days to work with her before I left. She previously worked as a juvenile probation officer and enjoyed writing social histories. Her eagerness to learn and her commitment to doing quality work were evident from the beginning.

Since my retirement, two more officers have joined District 26. The secretarial staff remains golden with Marion Dodson, Cynthia Collins, and Diane Fletcher, who replaced Pete Tanner. Collectively, they join Dan, Chip, and ACE to chart a new course.

In this new era, this group will face its own unique challenges and make their own memories. In time, I hope someone emerges to tell their story. Like mine and my colleagues', it will surely be worth telling.

CPSIA information can be obtained
at www.ICGtesting.com
Printed in the USA
LVOW04s1113070816
499259LV00002BB/4/P